THE SCATTERED PAPERS OF PENELOPE

ΛΕΕΙ Η ΠΗΝΕΛΟΠΗ

(Ἀπό Τά Σκόρπια Χαρτιά τῆς Πηνελόπης)

Δέν ὕφαινα, δέν ἔπλεκα,
ἕνα γραφτό ἄρχιζα, κι ἔσβηνα
κάτω ἀπ' τό βάρος τῆς λέξης
γιατί ἐμποδίζεται ἡ τέλεια ἔκφραση
ὅταν πιέζετ' ἀπό πόνο τό μέσα.
Κι ἐνῶ ἡ ἀπουσία εἶναι τό θέμα τῆς ζωῆς μου
— ἀπουσία ἀπ' τή ζωή —
κι γράμματα βγαίνουν στό χαρτί
κι ἡ φυσική ὀδύνη τοῦ σώματος
πού στερεῖται.

. . . .

κι ἐγώ μέ λέξεις θά λύσω
τίς μηχανές πού μέ δένουν
μέ τόν συγκεκριμένο ἄντρα
πού νοσταλγῶ
ὅσο νά γίνει σύμβολο Νοσταλγίας ὁ Ὀδυσσέας
καί ν' ἀρμενίζει τίς θάλασσες
στοῦ καθενός τό νοῦ.

Ἐξηγῶντας
πώς ὅ,τι χάνει σέ ἀφή
κερδίζει σέ οὐσία.

(1976-1977) Κατερίνα Ἀγγελάκη-Ρούκ

THE SCATTERED PAPERS OF PENELOPE
NEW AND SELECTED POEMS

Katerina Anghelaki-Rooke

EDITED BY
Karen Van Dyck

GRAYWOLF PRESS
Saint Paul, Minnesota

Publication of this volume is made possible in part by a grant provided by the Minnesota State Arts Board, through an appropriation by the Minnesota State Legislature; a grant from the Wells Fargo Foundation Minnesota; and a grant from the National Endowment for the Arts, which believes that a great nation deserves great art. Significant support has also been provided by the Bush Foundation; Target; the McKnight Foundation; and other generous contributions from foundations, corporations, and individuals. To these organizations and individuals we offer our heartfelt thanks.

A Lannan Translation Selection
Funding the translation and publication of exceptional literary works

The translator is also grateful for the additional support from the Greek Ministry of Culture and the Lodge Fund at Columbia University.

Published by Graywolf Press
2402 University Avenue, Suite 203
Saint Paul, Minnesota 55114

www.graywolfpress.org

Published in the United States of America

ISBN 978-1-55597-519-7

2 4 6 8 9 7 5 3 1
First Graywolf Printing, 2009

Library of Congress Control Number: 2008935601

Cover design: Christa Schoenbrodt, Studio Haus

Cover art: Portrait of the poet as Penelope, gift from the artist Alekos Fasianos.

CONTENTS

LIPIU

NEW POEMS

INTRODUCTION:
THE ISLAND OF RETURN

The Greek poet Katerina Anghelaki-Rooke calls the island Aegina the island of return. Only an hour from Athens by boat, the island's port is busy all year round. It is particularly packed in the summer months. In the cafés along the waterfront one finds a cosmopolitan mix of Athenian intellectuals, British beachgoers, Japanese tourists riding in brightly colored horse-drawn buggies and local fishermen taking a break from their nets. Back again for the summer, I walk through town, picking up a newspaper and a few *tirópites* (cheese pies). When I reach the big red house with the green shutters, I call up to Katerina's window. Pushing through the dogs and cats, I make my way to the kitchen where Rodney Rooke, the poet's husband of forty years, is listening to the BBC. I give him the newspaper and take the *tirópites* to the table in the pistachio grove. Katerina comes down the stairs in her flower print dress. She is over sixty-five, but the dark shiny hair flying around her shoulders and her jaunty syncopated gait make her seem younger. After kisses, she checks the time: before twelve, a coffee, after twelve, a beer. "Let's look over the translations," she says, "but first I have a joke to tell you." One joke leads to another, then there's a tale of some poet or politician who is in trouble and a tricky Greek expression to explain. Finally, there's a pause: "Do you want to hear my new poem?"

Katerina always has poems to share, sometimes a series, sometimes a whole collection. Inspiration is never something she hoards. There is more, lots more of it. Indeed the abundance of papers spread out on her desk is daunting: poems, essays, interviews, her journals and her own translations from Russian, French, and English. Penelope, it turns out, wasn't weaving, but writing. And the absence Penelope felt wasn't simply about Odysseus, but about her own attempt to turn absence into presence on the page. As she writes in one of her best-known poems:

I wasn't weaving, I wasn't knitting
I was writing something
erasing and being erased
under the weight of the word

> ("Penelope Says," *translated by Karen Van Dyck*)

Katerina begins to read her new poem aloud. As I listen I am re-minded again of the Penelope poem, in which composing a poem is as natural as daybreak:

and I begin again in the morning
with new birds and white sheets
drying in the sun.

> ("Penelope Says," *translated by Karen Van Dyck*)

This is the feat of her poetry: making the extraordinary ordinary. Her poems anchor the abstract metaphysics of myth in the rituals of everyday life.

I

When Katerina Anghelaki-Rooke was a year old, the celebrated writer and critic Nikos Kazantzakis stood as godfather at her baptism. When she was four, he taught her how to swim in the Aegean. When she was seventeen, he published her poem "All Alone" in an Athenian magazine with a note saying that it was the most beautiful poem he had ever read. By her early twenties she was already an established poet. During the dictatorship (1967–1974) she and a group of younger poets spearheaded a new kind of poetry that grappled with the confusion and censorship of those years. Meeting regularly with the translator Kimon Friar, they produced an anthology of six young poets, one of the first books to break the self-imposed silence initiated by the Nobel laureate poet George Seferis in response to the colonels' press laws. Anghelaki-Rooke is among the strong women poets who emerged from this experience. Linking the women poets of the previous postwar generation

(Eleni Vakalo, Kiki Dimoula) to those of the generation of the '70s (Rhea Galanaki, Maria Laina, Jenny Mastoraki), Anghelaki-Rooke stands out for the lyrical accessibility of her poetry. Having won the Greek National Prize for Poetry (1985) and the Greek Academy's Poetry Prize (2000), Anghelaki-Rooke is widely considered one of the major poetic voices in Greece today.

Kazantzakis and Anghelaki-Rooke share the important Greek family tie of godfather and godchild. They share their love for the island of Aegina, the sea, and travel. They share a literary tradition from Homer to Seferis. But here the similarities end. The problem that consumed Kazantzakis his whole life, the impossible meeting of body and soul, best illustrated in his novel *The Last Temptation of Christ,* is never an issue for Anghelaki-Rooke. Her poetry is a poetry of flesh, indiscretion, and the divine all rolled into one. Whereas for Kazantzakis the body is an impediment to spiritual fulfillment, for Anghelaki-Rooke it is a passageway. It is through the body that everything makes sense. As she told the Greek poet Panos Stathogiannis in an interview: "I do not distinguish the soul from the body and from all the mystery of existence . . . Everything I transform into poetry must first come through the body. My question is always how will the body react? To the weather, to aging, to sickness, to a storm, to love? The highest ideas, the loftiest concepts, depend on the morning cough . . ." (For the original Greek see *Helios: The Voice of Three Seas, Special Issue on Katerina Anghelaki-Rooke.* No. 6, June 2004).

The body, myth, history, nature, gender, and language are inextricably entangled concepts in Anghelaki-Rooke's poetry, but usually the body comes first. For her the body embraces a huge expanse of history and experience. As the title of an early poem declares, "The Body Is the Victory and the Defeat of Dreams." The body is not only her own, but contains the outside world, from the streets of the town to nature and beyond. Trees, mountains, and sky are in the gut, in the ears, nose, and mouth, between the toes, in our hair. In one poem a geyser is held between two lovers:

In the heat of Greece
our sternums pressed together
spurted water.
I drank your sweat
along with your kisses
your sigh
in the shade of the shutters.

("Heat," *translated by Katerina Anghelaki-*
Rooke and Jackie Willcox)

The intermixing of inner and outer worlds at times reaches such a
level that the body only exists as the body of another person. And
sometimes the other is not even human, but an animal—a moth
flapping around a lamp, a dog scratching her fleas in the shade. An
erotic conquest is imagined in terms of a spider and her prey; the
protection of the human soul, in terms of a polar bear fighting off
the cold with her layers of fat.

More often than not the body, someone else's or an animal's, is
female or viewed from a feminine perspective. Anghelaki-Rooke's
attention to women's experience does not lead to absolute state-
ments about the difference between the sexes, nor is it a nostalgic
nod to a mythical matriarchal past. It is a matter of the here and
now: "I don't know what will happen in two hundred years, but
for now it is difficult for women to express what is going on with
their own sex. For men, things are different. They have all of his-
tory behind them. . . . They have the luxury of writing about their
state, their nation, and their ideas. Women . . . still have a long way
to go. In poetry, they have not yet exhausted the topic of gender."
(*Helios*).

Anghelaki-Rooke's poetry reads Greek history and myth through
the female body, and yet it is not directed specifically at women
or at Greek readers. Parallel to the way Irish women poets such as
Eavan Boland use the figure of woman to speak about the problems
of a people, Anghelaki-Rooke takes her everyday experiences and
turns them into allegories of modern life for everyone. Her poetry

can be seen to fit into the tradition of the best of American feminist poetry, alongside Adrienne Rich and Anne Sexton, where writing the body and rewriting myth are central concerns. Anghelaki-Rooke's poetry, though, is less militant. Her Penelopes and Helens cook dinner for their husbands and suitors with one hand and write poetry with the other. Her brand of feminism is more one of daily practice than politics. It emerges from a culture in which women act differently from men and therefore write differently, a culture in which women are still more tied to the inner spaces of the home. Gender inequality is not so much an existential problem as a practical one.

This common sense approach pervades her view more generally of disability and physical difference. Men, women, dogs, all have their wounds. Women, historically, may have it tougher than men, and dogs and other animals may be even lower on the totem pole, but her point is that exceptions from the norm, any norm, whether socially constructed or painfully real, are a natural part of life. There is nothing freakish or otherworldly about imperfection. Her body, her poetry reveals, is not different just because it is female, but because it almost didn't survive. In a poem she describes her early fight to live:

> Instead of a star, a scar shone over my birth.
> The pain my uncongealed body suffered
> pushed me back into the original darkness.
> I crawled on nothingness, my tiny fingers
> clutching death like a shiny black toy.
> ("The Scar," *translated by Katerina Anghelaki-
> Rooke and Jackie Willcox*)

Here she is referring to a childhood illness that left her with a serious limp and a withered arm. The poet is fond of pointing out the historical irony that had she been born six months later, once penicillin had been discovered, she would have been fine. In her poetry the disfigured body is not a radically different body, but rather, as with the issue of being a woman, an ordinary part of the world and of history that has simply gone less noticed. Her assumption is that if these experiences are discussed more regularly, they will become more acceptable.

The sexual encounter provides a potent way to dissolve the difference between her body and the other bodies. Her infirmities prove quite adequate to the tasks of loving. In fact in one poem her misshapen hand has the upper hand:

> She sees her image
> as she sits and thinks about her lovers
> mentally she caresses their self deception
> with her withered hand.
>
> ("The Heroine Contemplates Her Hand,"
> *translated by Karen Van Dyck*)

Prosthetic devices, whether crutches or the bicycle she uses to get around Aegina, are useful additions to the body. In one poem, another addition, a dildo helps her understand how male power is not necessarily knowledge:

> "So, he knows nothing about me either when he shoves,"
> I thought as I stood alone leaning on the window sill. And
> the difference between the plastic and the real is only a
> somewhat greater resistance to time.
>
> ("My Plastic Thing," *translated by Katerina*
> *Anghelaki-Rooke and Jackie Willcox*)

II

Anghelaki-Rooke's poetry can be divided into periods in which her poems are grounded more in autobiography, others in which myth predominates and still others that are meditations on the act of writing itself. There seems to be an almost cyclical pattern to these periods. The poems in her early *Magdalene, the Vast Mammal* (1974) are the first sort with their attention to family genealogy, while the next two collections, *The Scattered Papers of Penelope* (1977) and the *The Triumph of Constant Loss* (1978), draw loosely on myth for their structure, turning the ancient Penelope into a modern woman poet. In the prose poems of *Counter Love* (1982) we find a self-reflexive moment of thinking about the process of writing followed by a return to the Penelope myth as the structuring principle in *The Suitors* (1984). Autobiography takes over again in *Epilogue Wind* (1990) and *Empty Nature* (1993), though here autobiography doubles as social commentary in the form of a diary about the first Gulf War. Myth then predominates again in *Flesh Is a Beautiful Desert* (1996), while the new poems of her most recent collections, *Matter Alone* (2001) and *Translating Life's End into Love* (2003), focus, in a more self-reflexive way, on what makes poetry poetry and the role of translation in this process.

As her poetry has matured, her concern for language has taken the place of her concern for the body. Language is not only the means, but, increasingly, the topic of her poems. The shift is felt in her two poems about an imaginary place of sadness called Lipiu. (The name uses the root of the word for sadness in Greek, *lípi,* and the Romanian suffix for places, *u,* to recall the fact that the poem was composed in the Romanian city of Sibiu.) The first, "Lipiu," describes the place and the bodies that inhabit it, while the second, "Lipiu Once Again," addresses the language that is spoken there.

> You read the trees, the mountains in the original.
> You ask: What do I have to say in this language?
> ("Lipiu Once Again," *translated by Karen Van Dyck*)

As the poet herself remarked, "All my life I've been saying that I serve poetry. Lately I have begun to see that what I am really doing is serving language. Poetry is the instrument, the medium. I have an almost religious attachment to language. I believe that when I say a phrase in English, I live and perceive reality in a different way than if I say the same thing in Greek" *(Helios).* Whereas her earlier poems tried to capture different kinds of pleasure and pain in poetry, over the last decade it has been the actual translation of this pleasure and pain into language that has concerned her most.

III

For obvious reasons, Anghelaki-Rooke's work is usually anthologized under titles that focus on the central role of the body in her poetry. Her first chapbook in English used the title of her poem "The Body Is the Victory and the Defeat of Dreams." A retrospective collection in Greek bore the title of another of her poems, "When the Body." Her French translator used the title of the collection *Flesh Is a Beautiful Desert*. I have taken a slightly different tack by choosing for my selection the title from the volume *The Scattered Papers of Penelope*, which puts the emphasis on myth, language, and the particular work of writing as a woman. With this title I want to call attention to how many of Anghelaki-Rooke's best poems, especially her more recent ones, address the issue of writing and experiment with different genres such as the prose poem or the diary entry. I want to stress how her poetry of the body is always also a poetry concerned with issues of gender and language. This title also alludes to my own task of putting into order the scattered translations of Anghelaki-Rooke. As this collection attests, Anghelaki-Rooke's poetry has been translated by some of the best translators of Greek poetry. These translations, however, exist in small press publications, out-of-print journals, poetry festival programs, or sometimes even unpublished in drawers, and are not available to the general reader. My job has been to gather up and then edit these translations together with the poet.

It is one thing to introduce a poet to readers in another language by describing a poetic project in critical terms and quite another to do so by editing a collection of translations, especially one that includes translations that are not all one's own. In the first case one can explain what gets lost in translation. In the second, the translations must speak for themselves. While a critic may relish the linguistic idiosyncrasies of a poet's work and discuss them at length, translators tend to shy away from them. Certainly the greatest challenge in bringing Anghelaki-Rooke's poetry into English is the rich variety of linguistic registers that are the everyday fare of Greek speakers. Ancient Greek proverbs as well as Byzantine liturgical phrases are still in daily use. Anghelaki-Rooke is a master of Greek's linguistic promiscuity. What to make of her words gathered from all corners of the Greek language as well as from other languages, and from all sorts of texts: literature, history, daily news reports, and advertisements? How does one capture in English snatches drawn from nineteenth-century romantic poets such as Solomos, Porfyras, and Malakasis, from Cavafy, or from her peers of the postwar generations like the lyrical Nikos Karouzos or the more meditative Andonis Fostieris? How to convey the echoes from poems by Rimbaud, Pushkin, Heaney, and Plath that she has translated from other languages? Ultimately what allows Anghelaki-Rooke to succeed in English translation is that, no matter what the source of her language, the dominant tone of her poems is conversational. The wild mix of registers almost always sounds to the reader like everyday speech, as if the poet were telling a joke or a story or relaying a dream she had the night before. In the final analysis it is this apparent ordinariness, I think, that makes her poetry translatable into English and that has made this collection of translations by different translators possible.

But this is not to say that her translators ignore Anghelaki-Rooke's linguistic inventiveness. The translations I have chosen fold into the translatable conversational tone some inkling of the untranslatable complex language-world the poet inhabits. They give the English speaker not only a sense of the seamlessness with which a poem ends and everyday conversation begins, but also a curiosity about where a word comes from and whether it really is a word we know or not.

Let me give one example. In the first "Lipiu" poem she writes:

> You arrive in Lipiu without a sigh
> only a slight tightening

like love standing
indecisive at the door.
Here you find cloud-stepping poets,
poets with an aptitude for heaven

("Lipiu," translated by Karen Van Dyck)

In Greek the adjective translated as "cloud-stepping" is one
Anghelaki-Rooke has made up—*ierovámones* (literally from sacred
iero and stepping *vaino*). In its structure, however, it recalls the real
word *aitherovámones* (heaven-stepping), which refers to people
who are caught up in their own thoughts, whose heads are in the
clouds. By invoking a real word in her made-up one, Anghelaki-
Rooke expresses both the absentmindedness and the divinity of
poets. The English "cloud-stepping" is an attempt to do the same.

Again I should emphasize that such word games are infrequent
and it is their infrequency that gives them their power. Anghelaki-
Rooke's linguistic playfulness should be distinguished from that
of a long tradition of surrealist and language-oriented poetry in
Greece. Hers, for example, is not the intricate punning of Kiki
Dimoula, who treats the Greek language like an acrobat balanc-
ing whole metaphysical arguments on a part of speech. "Mine,"
Anghelaki-Rooke clarified in conversation, "is different. If you
don't get it, you don't lose much. I am not interested in distorting
reality when I play with language."

To produce this collection of translations I went back through
her three volumes of collected poems as well as her more recent
books and chose the best translations available from each period,
making my own when I felt a certain poem was missing or was in-
adequately translated. I also tried to include different translators
when possible. I wanted the different Anghelaki-Rookes conjured
by Rae Dalven, Kimon Friar, and Edmund Keeley, some of whom,
like old friends, I had become very fond of and found it hard to do
without. I was also heartened to realize that a collection of trans-
lations by different hands did not preclude the possibility of a
recognizable voice. There is something about Anghelaki-Rooke's

poems that teaches their translators to write English in a certain way. At times one even wonders whether her life in many languages means that these poems are already partly thought out in English. Working with the poet, therefore, I could preserve a style by editing the translations and suggesting changes, a collaboration of sorts, at least with the living translators.

The present selection came into its own at a pivotal moment. On Anghelaki-Rooke's table three summers ago when I arrived in Aegina was a pile of her own English translations of her latest collection, *Translating Life's End into Love*. Was this supposed to be a sign that my work was over? Did she no longer need her English translators? Might this turn to English be a part of what "translating life's end into love" means? Could it be a prescient blueprint for how to live without her English husband who then passed away the next fall? Was it also an acknowledgment of the crucial role that translation between Greek and English plays in her own life and poetry? I close this collection with my translation of that book's title poem. It is both the newest of her new poems included here and an appropriate conclusion to a collection of English translations since with it she proposes that poetry itself is a matter of translation—from life's end into love, from love to the page, and from Greek into English.

Karen Van Dyck

MAGDALENE, THE VAST MAMMAL

The Body Is the Victory
and the Defeat of Dreams

The body is the Victory of dreams
when shameless as water
it rises from slumber
its pock marks, its scars
such signs still asleep
its dark olive groves
in love,
cool to the hand.

The body is the Defeat of dreams
spread out long and empty
(if you shout, you hear the echo)
with its anemic tiny hairs
unloved by time
wounded, sobbing
hating its own motion
its original black color
fades steadily
when it wakes it clasps its bag
hanging on to pain for hours
in the dust.

The body is the Victory of dreams
when it puts one foot in front of the other
and gains a certain ground.
A place.
With a heavy thump.
Death.
When the body gains a place
in the town square
after death
like a wolf with a burning snout

it howls "I want it"
"I can't stand it"
"I threaten—I revolt"
"My baby is hungry."

The body gives birth to justice
and its defense.
The body creates the flower
spits out the death-pit
tumbles over, takes flight
spins motionless around the cesspool
(the world's motion)
in dreams the body triumphs
or finds itself naked in the streets
in pain;
it loses its teeth
shivers from love
breaks its earth open
like a watermelon
and is done.

TRANSLATED BY *Karen Van Dyck*

Penelope Says

And your absence teaches me
what art could not
DANIEL WEISSBORT

I wasn't weaving, I wasn't knitting
I was writing something
erasing and being erased
under the weight of the word
because perfect expression is blocked
when the inside is pressured by pain.
And while absence is the theme of my life
—absence from life—
tears and the natural suffering
of the deprived body
appear on the page.

I erase, I tear up, I stifle
the living cries
"Where are you, come, I'm waiting for you
this spring is not like other springs"
and I begin again in the morning
with new birds and white sheets
drying in the sun.
You will never be here
to water the flowers
the old ceiling dripping
under the weight of the rain
with my personality
dissolving into yours
quietly, autumn-like . . .
Your choice heart
—choice because I have chosen it—
will always be elsewhere

and I will cut
with words
the threads that bind me
to the particular man
I long for
until Odysseus becomes the symbol of Nostalgia
sailing the seas of every mind.
Each day
I passionately forget you
that you may be washed of the sins
of fragrance and sweetness
and finally all clean
enter immortality.
It is a hard and thankless job.
My only reward is that I understand
in the end what human presence is
what absence is
or how the self functions
in such desolation, in so much time
how nothing can stop tomorrow
the body keeps remaking itself
rising and falling on the bed
as if axed down
sometimes sick, sometimes in love
hoping that what it loses in touch
it gains in essence.

TRANSLATED BY *Karen Van Dyck*

JEALOUSY

On Sundays he walks with that woman
and together they enjoy
the desolate countryside.
Look at them, they're passing by the farms:
under the hedge two dead pigs
stretch out their hooves to the afternoon
a light frost covers the mud
the snow has melted
but the earth is still speechless
all alone before becoming a butterfly.
Their love,
is it peace or is it torture?
Lemon sun.
Who is she?
What face?
What breast?
The countryside is slowly stuffed with night.
There's nothing exotic
in this geography and he
holds the woman with so much passion
as they slide like one body into the room.
He takes off his shirt
his long-suffering breast
smells of sweat and fresh air;
slowly the dry branches give way
to memory
and the landscape begins again inside them
in full spring.

TRANSLATED BY *Gail Holst-Warhaft*

THE SUITORS

From the window
the garden seems to belong
elsewhere
and the house to travel
on a leaf.
Through the window grille
the suitors of my silence
are cut into slices;
they meet and organize my life
as if it were a party
and the smell of cooking
from all those years of waiting
reaches me upstairs.
The suitors fly around me
dazzled by the light
of my blinding loneliness;
when I look at them from above
it is because I am in a room
filled with Odysseus.
I won't talk again
about his sublime voice
his slight originality
that from the beginning made him eternal
but about a change
a shining thread
inside me.
I reach the essence of myself
by waiting.
How can I describe the kernel
when it is no longer surrounded by anything
when it is naked, but not scared
when it shakes, but doesn't flail
when it imposes on me the steadfastness

of time?
A seriousness begins with me
and takes over all of nature.
If this continues
even death will have value.

　　　回

I hear the shouting downstairs,
I too once had
mud in my hair
lemon blossoms behind my ears
and would cry passionately
"Free yourself of your bonds!"
but the bonds go deep:
a way of being
where the self plays itself.
Now there's only one window;
behind it my little private shadow
my natural world.
Shut up in the house
as if in time
I look at the tree
as if it were God:
outside of time.
I understand something
about my presence
here
with you and separate from you;
my flesh waits for you
but my mind saw you coming
long ago
and has already accompanied you to the door.

Faces only exist
inside us
their eyes rowing
in our body fluids.

TRANSLATED BY *Karen Van Dyck*

THE TRIUMPH OF CONSTANT LOSS

The Triumph of Constant Loss

For Andonis Fostieris

We will never be
what we are at this brief moment
but this constant loss
is a triumph.
Only the silence
of the leaves is saved
the body grows dark
along with the day
up to the unexpected flash
of the black night.
Fragments of life
replace the colors
in the littler portrayals
of the dream,
scratches replace
the shadows of the light
on the temporary skin.
Blinded by so much darkness
I sought God
and they gave me only
one finger to rub myself with;
now I triumph
in the most secret places,
where the idea
is conceived: here,
I learn at last
that I will leave first.

TRANSLATED BY *Rae Dalven*

From THE ANGEL POEMS

II

Angels are the whores of heaven;
with their wings they caress the most peculiar
psychologies;
they know the secrets of egomania
when they call the leaf a tree
and the tree a forest.
"That's how God made us," they say, stooping,
as light pours like golden hair or laughter;
they hold their hats to their breasts
when they are saying goodbye
and enter into another,
a better world.
Only a peppery smell
remains
on the windowsill
and on the tongue a taste
of divine betrayal.

TRANSLATED BY *Kimon Friar*

III

He would emerge bodily out of snow
with red on the tip of his little tongue
and white movements
that abolished white.
He would say to me, look,
love one day will become
a disposition only,
a disposition toward a snowflake;
the heart will steady itself for a moment
lightly on something the least solid . . .
Slowly, very slowly, you will notice
that all of beauty is but a falling
of water
of leaf
of snow . . .

Later, he washed himself with myrrh
and smelled of the precious
soaps of heaven.
In the basement where we lived
the dog had gutted the pillow
and ice had plugged
all openings.
He fell upon me, white and light,
and I was only a surface
without any of the hollows
where passion stagnates;
morality spread out on my skin
like ointment, and I too emitted the elusive
odor of nothingness.
I heard my heart

trapped with his kindness,
and from his eyes of turquoise
the liquids of his compassion
dripped in my palms.
Our difference, he told me,
as he caressed my incurable tentacles,
lies in consciousness.
Wings bear witness
to perfect loss.
When love shall become
a vague breeze
that imprints itself as only
the swaying of a leaf,
then the dark cumuli of your soul
shall turn you into snow
and you shall softly rejoice in love
to its last frozen
drop.

In my mouth the angel's thought
is still a body;
it throbs and hurls
death.

TRANSLATED BY *Kimon Friar*

V

Before they ripen into diffused spirits,
angels are leaf-stalks
and their wings begonia leaves
with dark surfaces
and red glitterings within.
Slowly, very slowly, they emerge out of the flowerpot
of the body,
take on the face of Bill or Bob,
pierce through the cool bower
of the world
and ascend like the promise
of a harmonious end;
on their lips shine
the last bubbles of our breathing,
those droplets
of our unrelieved loneliness.

TRANSLATED BY *Kimon Friar*

VII

When an angel grows red
and walks on tiptoe
on the well-scrubbed white,
believing in his inner flame
and airing it out of the window,
this is because he has fallen so much in love
with worldly things
that he avoids comparing them
with those in heaven.
Neither I nor anyone else
know what dangers
lie lurking for him
behind kitchen curtains
clay flower pots
and swollen-bellied girls
when their glances stray
into their inner
chaos pregnant with hope.
As for me, I only know
the babbling of the commonplace
when my dear aunt
is deified by death:
like a slim spider
she puts her closets in order,
myopically adoring their contents.

When the angel
turns ultramarine toward evening
and finishes his cigarette,

he will leave.
He will have conquered the temptation,
the magical spell,
that season after season
induces him
submissively to await his dying.

TRANSLATED BY *Kimon Friar*

Interlude

Honest are angels, honest,
for even when
they blind you with whiteness
they whisper "I don't exist."

TRANSLATED BY *Kimon Friar*

VIII

When angels chance to become
lovers, they offer themselves
with a hard shell on the outside
that keeps them untouchable
amid the evils of passion.
I caress the uneven surfaces
of their carapaces
and resemble a blind woman,
run my fingers up and down
to find some opening as at midnight
they silently extend a member,
a dark extension of themselves
that searches me out as I envelop them.
My senseless company seems headless
and so I feel free
to imagine angels
with wide-spread wings
sunning themselves on their backs
in the divine scorching heat
with their fleshy jewels
glittering in the air.

TRANSLATED BY *Kimon Friar*

X

If in nature Being becomes secure
and ceases to whirl about,
if it conceives of change without moving,
the angel will raise frame high
and the image will spread out like a rug
and transport us.

TRANSLATED BY *Kimon Friar*

COUNTER LOVE

I Have a Stone

I lick a stone. The pores of my tongues fuse with the pores of the stone. My tongue grows dry and creeps to the side of the stone which touches the ground where mould sticks to it like blood. Suddenly the saliva flows again, moistens the stone, and the stone rolls into my mouth.

I call this stone Oedipus. It too is irregular, with deep grooves for eyes. It too rolls down with swollen feet. And when motionless it hides a fate, a reptile, my forgotten self.

I call this stone Oedipus.

Although by itself it has no meaning, it too has the shape and the weight of choice. I name it and I lick it.

Until the end of my story.

Until I understand what choice means.

Until I understand what the end means.

TRANSLATED BY *Katerina Anghelaki-Rooke and Jackie Willcox*

HEAT

In the heat of Greece
our sternums pressed together
spurted water.
I drank your sweat
along with your kisses
your sigh
in the shade of the shutters.
There as the violent afternoon
came on, you too were ablaze
with your tangled hair
your divine lashes
your laughter refracted
through the salty prisms of passion.
In the sizzling heat
in the total stillness—
the only shadow above us
black as destiny—
the outline of our existence
an equation of insects.
August festered
like an open sore
while relentless cicadas
echoed the poet's
closing lines.
Not a breath of air . . .
The pedantic fly that defiles everything
sits on your cock
drinking your sap.
The watermelon-man
passes with his megaphone.

The afternoon
falls at my feet
like a severed head.

TRANSLATED BY *Katerina Anghelaki-Rooke and Jackie Willcox*

THE CICADA

Thousands of summer songs accumulate inside me. I open my mouth and in my passion, try to put them in order. I sing. Badly. But thanks to my song I stand out from the branches and from other voiceless sound-boxes of nature. My simple dress—gray and lime-white—bars me from every excess of aestheticism and so, cut off from the rowdy festival of time, I sing. I ignore Spring, Easter and violets. The only resurrection I know is when a faint breeze manages to stir and slightly cool the burning heat of my life. Then I stop howling—or, as the world thinks, singing—because the miracle of coolness deep inside me says more than all I create so as not to die of heat.

TRANSLATED BY *Gail Holst-Warhaft*

My Plastic Thing

It was plastic. That member, that foreign organ. I wore it and felt nothing. I just shoved. The world was hard and elastic at the same time. When my movements were artful enough, there was no resistance. And all that came back to me from the tight passage of the other body was the shiver of the conquered earth. No knowledge. Only stupid power. And there I was, expecting knowledge! "So, he knows nothing about me either when he shoves," I thought as I stood alone leaning on the window sill. And the difference between the plastic and the real is only a somewhat greater resistance to time. But power. . . . No, not power . . . violence. Violence and the annihilation of the other are one and the same. Annihilation.

TRANSLATED BY *Katerina Anghelaki-Rooke and Jackie Willcox*

WRITING

The obscene gesture I make when I take up my pen, while something stirs in the slight breeze: the skin of my nature. As when the poor soul slowly raised his arm and surrounded me with modest glory, his gurgling voice like that of a child's reciting heroic verses before being put to death. His hand with its bitten nails slowly entered me until I became the motion of my own burial. That contact ended each poem. I bring my table and my papers to this new erotic landscape. I get down to writing. I set the machinery in motion. By the third line my new inspirer has totally conquered me. I understand how he lives and how he saps me. My imaginings begin to be more than my actions. My hands sweat. I put down my pen, wipe the three fingers holding it on my fat thighs. Creation's in full swing.

TRANSLATED BY *Katerina Anghelaki-Rooke and Jackie Willcox*

THE LITTLE LADDER

My body is a little ladder that I lean against the wall of the world. I climb up it, I stretch myself to look behind the wall, behind the four walls of feeling. The little ladder keeps shaking more and more, I scorn it more and more, and I want to let myself go to the view of the gardens without any sense of direction. For days I think of the deep earth's copulation that sprouts the grass and all the roots of this shameless vegetation. I look but I grow weary. The little ladder keeps shaking and the lights that illuminate the park become milky and then it is night. At the end of a specific but an unknown number of years, I will have forgotten all these chaotic gymnastics. I will be the warped little ladder that someone forgot leaning against the garden wall.

TRANSLATED BY *Rae Dalven*

MATCHSTICKS

Gulliver

who woke in the field, pinned to the earth like the lilies, fastened
like the ears of wheat, screwed down even by the finest hairs in his
nose, stuck like an insect in an entomologist's notebook, panicking
as he saw how the great bulk of his body was the terrain for millions
of brilliant enterprises carried out by tiny people who with match-
sticks and threads had reduced him to immobility

it's me

with my Lilliputian frenzied loves that keep me bound to the most
cloddish conception of life, the most constrained movement, to a
base apprehension of beauty as a body which undresses and lies
down and never rises to the skies.

TRANSLATED BY *Gail Holst-Warhaft*

Beings and Things on Their Own

Beings, when we leave them on their own, what are they like? What do they do when we stop fingering them, tickling them, biting them? When they are alone in their lather or in the mud of night?

Things, when we don't shove them between our legs, when we don't open them, don't close them, don't wear them and wait, don't take them off and wait, when we don't plan a weekend, a stroll, a vision, a show; when the snow remains untrodden by the beloved dog, the flowerpots in the forever-closed windows of our souls, what are they like? What is the world like when we are not there?

TRANSLATED BY *Katerina Anghelaki-Rooke and Jackie Willcox*

The Barber Shop

A white rose,
the barber's towel
around your face
shining like a beetle
clinging to the petals.
Clippings scattered on the floor
were the days when I loved you so much
while the garrulous
sculptor of heads cuts away
what time had made superfluous.
Ah! that unscrupulous hand made you
even more beautiful,
the curve of your eyebrows more clearly defined
and beneath the jade of your eyes,
your flowers, your lips half opened.
The shop impressed itself on my mind
in all its detail
and little by little the nothingness
which my life would soon become
without you
came crawling
into the scented room.
You smiled in the mirror
and I crumbled
because I had you and would lose you
like life classically cut short
by a pair of ancient scissors.

TRANSLATED BY *Katerina Anghelaki-Rooke and Jackie Willcox*

When the Body

When the body
promises itself
and fulfills its promise
desiring with voices
that spill into the garden and stick to the branches
like resin
when the body in its exaltation announces
"In chaos I exist absolutely"
and under the bare light of the bulb
splits in two
so that one half sinks into
the other half
when its word becomes
a perpendicular line
connecting it to the heavens
when the body
poisoned by juices
swaddled by touches
reveals itself to be all alone
and bedazzled
when it swallows what it gives out
when its gives in to what presses in
when its measured surface
has been measured countless times
by the eye, the mouth
the exacting lens of time
down to the last pimple, pore
when the beautiful proportions
curl up out of breath
and the argument
I am in love therefore I exist
is exhausted
the voices come back to the roots of the kidney

and a bird hidden
untouched by all the saliva and kisses
flies away, flies over
the desert space
sown with the teeth and hair
left behind by the body
when the body . . .

TRANSLATED BY *Karen Van Dyck*

THE SPIDER'S DREAM

So I take them to my place: an airy chamber with little breezes amidst tiny threads. I show the beautiful males to the couches of emptiness while I, round, at the center, deliver food to all who enter. In awe, I feed their flame from the abyss as their organs, bulging in their natural prisons, extend out to the web. My villa is built from the body's white energy and everything confirms the indestructible nature of my erotic scheming, while their ephemeral cries of pleasure die out down below where I began my ascent. The ending is familiar: the disappearance of the trapped erotic object and the eternal return of the insatiable spider. But in the irreversible horror of my victory, I dream of the invulnerable male who will eat me up. Smiling carelessly among the dead moths I imagine the winged cavalier with his antenna-embraces breaking me of the comfortable habit of killing, and there at the edge of the web slowly destroying me. With my skin shining from the secretions of my omnipotent passion I pour more and more thread into the mouth of the unexpected exploiter of my wise plot until I topple down from the heights of my gluttony, and give myself completely to my erotic executioner.

TRANSLATED BY *Karen Van Dyck*

SLEEP

At night
dreams spread over us
with all the horror of life;
you hold me tight, you call me,
a couple drowning, embracing
abreast the last wave.
The beauty we worshipped
is a fanciful curtain
pulled back at night
it is the threat surrounding bodies
and all the half-finished acts of the day
return to finish us off
in the dark.
I envy those people with neuroses and phobias
whom a scratch, a shadow, a suspicion
totally consumes.
I have nothing but death
simple, clear, round
a certainty
that sits on my chest.
You sleep next to me
without a wrinkle on your face
like a spring mast
sailing through sleep.
I touch you
and as your cool breath
caresses the roof of the dream
I find a little more sun, more water
before in a coma

the interminable return
to the root of the perishable
begins.

TRANSLATED BY *Karen Van Dyck*

THE SUITORS

THE THIRD SUMMER, OR THE CATASTROPHE

The house had fallen into a sweet sleep,
stone doors, a calcified soul
that always internally inhabits itself
while outside the steadfast owl
praises the deep end of night.
It was the third summer
that the same small individual had appeared,
a profligate part of this universal beauty
that defines and remains indefinable.
"Open your eyes," said the evil forebodings,
"look at the bushy tails of the animals,
see how straggly they become with time
and how what you adored under
the mandarin trees
furtively crosses the threshold."

Something makes us and we make
the walls one by one, all around
and in the middle we place the hearth
and the bridal chamber, the orange juice
on the bedside table.
It's not private property; we invite the light
to enter, to talk
about the meanings and the shadows
it has grasped and is contemplating alone.
But the bitter, incurable geraniums know
that what nourishes the symbols
of eternal well-being, also feeds the beasts with fierceness.
Deceptive kindness, these summer days,
the expansive immunity of blue is harsh
and the thoughts that go to cool themselves in the water
sink in the depths.

And this unimpeded nature
never goes forward in time;
it even braces itself in enmity
if it's about to flower.
Sometimes you say that nothing
ripens any more and at the time of flowering
madness poisons it all.
And those who beat
or set things on fire
were worshipped once;
they would sit naked in the shade
on the canvas chair
wearing a belt of kisses around their waists
with the devotee's string of blessings
down to the crack, there where all jealousies
merge with cries.
And so the guest of my body
leaves the cool seat;
the fingers that playfully rested
on the bathing suit become vulture's claws
love is transformed into an evil beast.

Spiteful night. Only once the honeysuckle
and his tongue dipped deep
into the well of delight.
Now catastrophe blew through the house
the crazed furniture rose
on its edges, its corners, its curves
then tumbled into the chasm of dream;
I fell too, came to pieces,

a lifeless crate
with my nails all over the floor
my teeth strewn.

TRANSLATED BY *Gail Holst-Warhaft*

EPILOGUE WIND

THE RED MOON

Behind the drab curtains of the trees
—something between the color of violent fertility and rotten
meat—the red moon rises now like fear all alone.
The dog, with his stomach heavy from all the tenderness
of my barren heart, empties his guts on the black earth.
The house is mute, gagged with guilt-gauze, memory-gauze;
blond women smile and disappear under the broken
plaster. Naked men become melancholic in the emptiness of
     the night.
Everything breathes heavily as if drunk on hemlock
while paralysis spreads slowly like silver light on paving-stones.
Suddenly life feels like a dungeon
and every season starts anew its own destruction.
In the speechless pain of the animal the trembling moment arose;
rarely had anyone such little hope.
The grass smelled of tears and as spring came on
from somewhere . . . the pine, sunk
in its dark future, was barely impressed by the yellow flowers.
A barbarian wind picked up
like a hasty lover with no imagination
and all the poems that I had heard in my life
came back from far away to bury me.
And it was as if I were traveling by train
leaving behind the land of merriment
and my body was entering a black forest.
The suffering dog was to blame, and those poems
that were wandering in the garden like ghosts;
they were different when I knew them,
when an angel, probably yellow by now
would cover them with long fingers and pour
an unmelting perfume on the provisional lines.
Now it seems like an hallucination that things eternal
as stone condescended to play a role

in the romantic scenes of our life. Fear has risen
a red putrefaction. It's gone too far, you say to yourself,
but you, you closed your eyes.

TRANSLATED BY *Karen Van Dyck*

From THE NARRATIVE OF THE SELF

The Scar

Instead of a star, a scar shone over my birth.
The pain my uncongealed body suffered
pushed me back into the original darkness.
I crawled on nothingness, my tiny fingers
clutching death like a shiny black toy.
I don't remember how I came to blossom into a wound,
how I learned to find a balance between pus
and my open eyes.
But at the point where my mother had assumed
that like a leaf on the water I'd be carried off
on my first journey by the stream of death,
she unexpectedly saw me emerge from the dark.
Who knows what exchanges were made that night,
what I gave and what I took, what I renounced,
what I promised so life would keep me in its service?
Was it blackmail, agreement or threat?
Should I be grateful for the butchered gift of existence
or vengeful? Had I been ordered
to look up or to cast my eyes down
to the roots of forgiveness?
Forgiveness? For what? What was this crushing weight
that had exhausted me
even before I had set off?
Or had I taken up another burden
that I'd carry limping to the end?

I lived and I began to play.
Trustingly I leaned upon the brace
and climbed the stairs.
In the attic I built the kingdom of my dreams
with paper cut-outs. I called it Florence,

my magic city, with its delicate ladies and gentlemen in hats.
Next to the door stood the water-tank
that thundered now and then
above the insubstantial actions of my heroes.
The warmth of this world drifted up from below,
the kitchen filled with smells, familiar sounds,
household voices: What time is it? Have you peeled the potatoes?
The kitchen and my paper imagination—
can the two poles of my existence have been fixed so early?

TRANSLATED BY *Katerina Anghelaki-Rooke and Jackie Willcox*

Aegina

Returning home from the sea my mother and I
always stopped to rest under the same olive tree.
She would tell me the tale of the ant and the cicada,
first lessons in restraint and wisdom,
while above our heads the poet shrieked
with passion in the sizzling heat.
Mother, what winter do you mean,
what misfortunes, what cold and hunger?
The miracle is this, it starts with the heat,
ends as soon as day enters the shadows:
the seeds are surrounded on all sides,
it's the ant who finds them
while the mindless grey creature falls silent and freezes.
Poor mother, you gave birth to a cicada
who's incapable of hoarding.

At daybreak I would sneak out of bed.
Dragging my nightgown over plants and ditches
I saw the garden as an endless domain,
the hens important personages absorbed in their pecking.
Time in the summer had no meaning,
the field was eternity, the water wheel turned its infinite round.
I dived into the hay, rolled
between the horse's legs; all joys
ended at the sea and there new ones began.
Even then I had fashioned two selves, the one sitting peaceful
and snug and well-disposed to all around,
the other thrilled by the danger an unknown body hides.
I called the winter peace, the summer madness
and turned into an angel in winter, a devil in the heat.
Mother was shocked by my two natures,

I blame the two worlds, she said,
the apartment block and the island.
But winter is coming soon,
what can she do. . . she'll have to settle down.

TRANSLATED BY *Katerina Anghelaki-Rooke and Jackie Willcox*

The Piglet

"You'll go far if the little piglet
doesn't eat you on the way."
My mother would often repeat the old French saying
and I always kept its image in my head
as if it were really right behind me.
It grunted and ran behind me smacking its porky lips.
Its skin was a patchwork of my shortcomings
and on its back the largest patch,
my passion for you.
With its strange legs, thick and aching,
it trampled on my lost moments
as they sank into your eyes, divine and cursed.
Now and then life offered me a focus, some meaning,
and the stumpy quadruped would lose ground.
I've beaten you, I cried, and high above
my mother appeared, flying over me like a bird,
like a little cloud.
But soon the pig would bite my heel again
and my consoling mother would disappear
together with her chair, her knitting.
Night, fed only by remorse, would take me,
again the dappled porker was triumphant
and off we'd set, inseparable, downhill.

TRANSLATED BY *Katerina Anghelaki-Rooke and Jackie Willcox*

Epilogue Wind

The wind lifts our sins into the air,
whirls them around for awhile high above
our idiotic schemes,
and lets them fall again to earth
where they blossom.
It gathers up the little words still damp,
you over there, come here,
and places them on the tops
of optimistic trees,
then spreads them on the ground
like dried souvenirs of nothing.
The wind lifts the torn leaves
of a short novella
and as they rise up, the page of our life
becomes legible, to be read someday in the future
like a meaning that is given to us whole.

Iowa (USA) 1974—Aegina 1989

TRANSLATED BY *Karen Van Dyck*

THE WEDDING

For Karen and Nelson on their wedding day

The wedding springs from the waters of youth
all cool separating the leaves of time;
like a wind-footed deer sniffing the air
or like fresh rain making the heavy sadness
of nature lighter.
It is a breeze that cools the embrace
of the sizzling hot day
it is a wreath made of blood and ideas.
The wedding is silence with the ear of the soul
listening attentively to the inner whisperings, the inner rituals.
The wedding is the guardian of the treasure of children's tears
sworn enemy of desolation and arrogance.

The wedding, the walking . . .

The wedding steps softly and embraces you from behind;
it covers your eyes with its hands and asks:
"Who am I?"
The wedding of life with what is beyond life
The wedding of life with its explanation
The wedding, the glorification of the perishable.
The wedding, the victory of the fragile
The wedding, the eternity of what is barely there
it comes as a hope for that feeling of goodness . . .

Oh, may it nestle always down there
where flaming birds
and purple flowers emerge!

The belly is the kingdom of the wedding
with the umbilical sanctuary in the middle.

That's where the wedding moves around and thinks
and cries and is fed
and grows up.
Here it forgets the ritual
here it studies and learns the books of the flesh
the lives of the married saints,
the documents with the official seals
—bites, kisses—
of love, all these ultimatums
with their victims and hostages.

If only we knew where the wedding came from,
how it's always in our homes
that it takes root and grows;
in the past it had alters and secret fires
now it stumbles dizzy in the busy streets.
The wedding, who brought it, what for?
and the bodies, why do they hold it so tightly between
    their chests?
The man purifies himself before it and his tears flow
and the woman forgets all the dark corners
of her fate, all her struggles
round like a sphere that equals "forever"
she touches the nape of his neck with her palm
they're heading toward children
under the roof of the knowledge-oath
the offering of essence
the right to happiness

the crashing defeat of sadness
for one flawless timeless moment

the wedding shines.

Pelion, 18 August 1989

TRANSLATED BY *Karen Van Dyck*

From SPRINGTIME FOR YANOUSA

Yanousa Counts Her Belongings

Can I be seen better in light or darkness?

Nature wears down slowly
in the eyes of the woman
who sits motionless in her chair
like a raindrop on a leaf.
Yanousa is at that point in life
where nothing progresses
and nothing happens suddenly.
She is inside everything and always left out;
everything nourishes her and she is no longer nourished.
Who's gone? Who'll come? Silence.
She begins to count. She has a garden.
There's the school beyond the trees
and then the sea.
She has a dog. And a close relation.
Days go by. She brings in very little money.
Today the earth drinks and drinks. A good rain.
Will the buds open, she wonders, will the branches grow heavy?
How many more times will she see this,
forty-nine years old, once a force to behold?

TRANSLATED BY *Karen Van Dyck*

The Heroine Contemplates Her Hand

I have a big one and a small one . . .

She has an unclear image
of herself
but him, she can see clearly
imprisoned in his underwear.
She knows his misery:
to exist as if he were someone else.
That's where she gets them all
at the edge of sorrow.
Sometimes they are beautiful and weak
sometimes they are rough and strong
They let her touch them,
because only she knows
how their other self excites them.

On the black window pane
—night, silence . . . the only sound
the garbage trucks chewing garbage—
she sees her image
as she sits and thinks about her lovers.
Mentally she caresses their self deception
with her withered hand.

TRANSLATED BY *Karen Van Dyck*

The Squirrel Replies to the Woman

I touched you in your sleep and you were warm . . .

I also jump
from imagination to deprivation
and all my searching for food
—even when in vain—
is accompanied by fluffy movements.
But on black days
when unreachable heights
become the only unbearable truth,
the rodent in me reveals itself
and mocks the sky blue room
I try to cross.
I only have one exercise left to learn,
I say to give myself courage: memory.
If I can remember the inner history
of fruit, I can have its taste again
without slicing it open.
Because memory and dream are the same in animals.
Look how at dusk
they poke their furry faces in the leaves,
deep in the sand, under the earth
and grow silent in the water.
In the heavenly calm of their thoughts
poetry comes out of its hiding place
and walks among them.
Then they dream or remember
their nasty, pointed enemy
running innocently across the waves
and all the food of nature
shining naked,

uncovered.
They sleep and remember,
they wake up and forget,
but they are always making
the twenty-four hour poem that is their life.

If we could separate poetry
from our sad bodies,
we would find it in the sleep of animals.

TRANSLATED BY *Karen Van Dyck*

Monastic

I knew rolls and rolls of black were waiting to wrap me.

The monk looked into her mouth
all empty, no teeth, no kisses.
His black hat
stained the blue sky
and his serenity was full of folds
like heavy silk in Dutch paintings.
Yanousa imagined
the hours of his salvation
dipped in oil and silence
and in lonely walks
along the edge of temptation's dew-fresh precipice.
And like the polar bear
with her body's fat-vision
endures the cold by imitating death
in her frozen hole,
the monk's soul
in the grey sack of his mind
imitates the absolute
in order to endure life.
At night with the moon
only his sobs are heard
and a cracking sound
as he kneels.

TRANSLATED BY *Karen Van Dyck*

Yanousa and a Poem

When I was in love, it flowered.

The sun a distant white flower
perfumed the cold.
Yanousa begins a poem.
She sees it stretching like the gum
we chewed as children
stretching out the window
and disappearing around the corner of the blue sky.
What was the poem about?
She forgot. Some memory that also disappeared
around the corner of the mind.
Why do people write poems?
So they have them when nature turns off the light.

TRANSLATED BY *Karen Van Dyck*

Even Raphael Is Helpless

I was holding love like a knife
stabbing ugliness into beautiful immobility.

Raphael climbs the hill dragging
the wind behind him.
A long time ago he had painted
the low stone wall that separated him
from the earth and he had drawn
the leaves spinning in the air before they fell.
He had illustrated his life
that separated him from heaven
as he went toward the mean-hearted
houses with their tall windows
and his eye took in
the stones one by one
like pink breasts.
But how sad that the wind
and his cough and the indigent trees
are more real
than all the dazzling Madonnas
born of his multi-colored mind,
while his black destiny
is more striking than the sky-blue fates
the women-consolers,
who emerge
from his paint box.

TRANSLATED BY *Karen Van Dyck*

Out of Her Life

I'm nowhere, but I'm not complaining . . .

Out of her life
another life emerges
even more uncertain
than the one before
with voiceless animals standing around
looking at her body
as if it were a well with a little bit of water
left at the bottom.
No fear stops her
not even death;
she puts it in a place
where she will never be.
But what's more important
is if at the end she manages
to keep something from nature
the way you struggle
to grasp the rhythm of your lover
and then in a single gesture
you both end up nowhere
back at the sea of "I am."
Thanks to the versatility
that such extreme exercise offers
the ashen woman hidden in time
receives a spring message
from a few silent flowers.

1986–1989

TRANSLATED BY *Karen Van Dyck*

IN THIS HOUSE SETTLING TIME'S ACCOUNT

1

I came back home
from Barbara's mansion.
The dazzling marble
had entombed my mind,
but when I saw the red
walls of a whole lifetime
I breathed again, though time
lies heavy with its own conscience here.

2

They're both up there now,
the two old men in the photograph.
Or perhaps they're still strolling
in the garden on their slender walking-sticks.
Indomitable shadows cross the threshold
and find me taking the air
on the balcony
passing an invisible thread
through the eye of the needle
that once stitched me.

3

"The moon, the moon!"
We stopped talking
about the old days—fresh-faced girls then
on our shining bicycles,
untamed, entangling in our wheels
our mothers' voices—
and parted the branches

to reveal the moon in its entirety,
like a yellow lid
on a transparent jar.

4

One was a widow, the other childless.
Through the night they unfolded their lives
laughing loudly at the sexual episodes.
Behind their chairs rose the moon
that had so often melted
like luminous butter on their bodies.
By the time it set, one had reached the part
about the funeral, the other about the hemorrhage.
At the door: "Let's not lose touch
now we've found each other again."

5

The house sucks at memories
and grows.
And like bricks indiscernible
beneath the plaster
the moving bodies
of the past support
in equal measure the weight
of the roof.

6

Last night I dreamt of a gigantic
nest of rats
beneath the stairs.

I smashed it and the house
deflated and collapsed
parachute-like on the ground.
The rats surrounded me
in alarm, for they too
had failed to see the elevated purpose
they had served.

7

There was a time when the two-story house
dominated here.
Now from their concrete terraces
the neighbors observe me
as, exposed, I water the plants,
feed the cats and the dogs,
hobbling moonstruck,
untutored in the future.

8

The power suppliers
came with new appliances
to increase the light
so I'd be abundantly illuminated
as I went down.
But in the dark I reckoned up
their charges.
"Thanks all the same," I said,
"I'm not interested."

9

Stones that never fall sick,
branches that always come back into bloom,
this is the scene that keeps
advancing toward the center.
Its views carry weight and
surreptitiously it takes the leading role.
I ask: what will the house think
when it sees me crawling
on the flagstones, begging
a few hours more in its shade?

10

Outside my window the rampant
mastic tree keeps eating up the sky.
Once its leaves barely
rested their eyes
on the window-sill, edging the view around.
My end will drip resin, I thought,
as I hang exhausted
from a thin blue cord.

TRANSLATED BY *Katerina Anghelaki-Rooke and Jackie Willcox*

EMPTY NATURE

WAR DIARY

13th Day, or Dry Land at Last!

The air battles come down to the ground
and death returns to earth,
the place of his origin.
High flashes accompany him,
the only luxury left for corpses.
How truly evil has changed direction!
His instantaneous action began from below
from the mud, hooves of animals,
army boots, swamps, and rose
to the black clouds and innocent little souls.
Now in the desert,
as I imagine her with countless
pink sandy breasts
breathing in the simoom,
a secret body
with its dark oases hidden down there below
unconcerned, a spectator at the catastrophe
who has turned into a parachutist to conquer her.
From above downwards now
the progress of bloody flesh;
the sky, a flaming past,
will be forgotten
and the good will be forced into the earth,
buried deep, very deep in memory.

TRANSLATED BY *Gail Holst-Warhaft*

14th day, or The Elimination of the Inner World

I am a grain of sand
swept along by the black waters.
The land flooded and the boundaries
between the two worlds were lost;
the inner, where memories germinated
together with weed-fears, moss-hopes
and the outer, drowned in the filthy effluent
of the latest news bulletins.
When was the dam breached?
Lava, sewers, manure
flow unimpeded inside me,
my inner life has been eliminated.
I tell myself to grab hold of a little branch of tenderness,
to remember your birthday
years ago in a snowy landscape . . .
But your body on mine
weighs me down like so many of the dead
and those eyes of yours
were described to me by inconsolable mothers
their color—like a lizard's shiver—
was painted for me by weeping girls
and wounded boys.
How was I plundered like this
without moving an inch from my room
and how did the flower bed of my grief
when I watched you leave
turn into the mass grave of the dead?
How is it that there where I had embroiled myself

in the skirmishes of the visible and the invisible
I wound up a fanatic spectator
of newsreel horror?

TRANSLATED BY *Gail Holst-Warhaft*

15th Day, or The Lesson

For Pedro Matteo

We said we'd have a lesson again today
as if there weren't. . . as if there weren't . . .
we, humans, without "power"
"the mandate of the people"
or some "sacred duty" to perform.
Language, we said,
language is an eternal tease!
What does *máscara* mean in Spanish?
"More face!" How funny!
Words—small surprises
with their simple meanings, their complex work . . .
But our laughter was suddenly cut off;
we thought of how even language
sounded too strange these days . . .
Night fell, we switched on the light
to see how glum we had become.
Reality teaches the most profound lessons
and knowledge is at first a heavy cloud
that assaults you,
before it becomes a light sheet
to cover you.

TRANSLATED BY *Gail Holst-Warhaft*

16th Day, or The End of the Person

I was going toward sleep
with my head full
of the smoke of scorched earth,
while unseen pincers
squeezed my heart.
And there, where every evening
I imagine the end of my person,
just like others say their prayers,
tonight I found that the war had left
a present on my pillow:
the meaninglessness of my death.

TRANSLATED BY *Gail Holst-Warhaft*

17th Day, or One More Elegy

All quiet on the front today,
only they didn't tell us how many
scorched men were buried in the sand.
I asked myself if the desert
rejects foreign bodies
as our own wretched body does . . .
Night falls; I read letters from the Interwar period;
they correspond and kiss each other with words
without knowing if they will ever see one another,
Tsvetayeva, Pasternak, Rilke.

TRANSLATED BY *Gail Holst-Warhaft*

18th Day, or The New Order of Things

I dreamed
that I found myself in the old love nest,
but everything had changed;
walls had crumbled,
new rooms had sprung up
whiter than lilies
with nurses all in white
who invited me to come inside.
"You know, I used to come here years ago . . ."
I said as if asking forgiveness,
while my eyes licked the corner
where the mattress once was.
Now it looked like the smudge of an eraser
in a child's exercise book
or like the snout of a wild boar
buried in green mildew
on an ancient stone.
A perfectly sweet smell wafted out of there
that didn't remind the woman once lying there
of anything any more.
"The new order of things,"
I murmured as I woke.

TRANSLATED BY *Gail Holst-Warhaft*

19th Day, or What We Know about Sleep

"We don't know where the knowledge
of sleep is based,"
said the learned professor on television
—between two assaults in the Gulf—
and he added that the more minute the animal
the less it sleeps.
Look at the bird
that hangs onto a high branch;
it knows
that if it should fall asleep there,
numbed by the divine blue,
it will drop down,
the branch will break,
and who knows into what fathomless embraces
of the dead it will fall,
if the bird should sleep soundly like that,
if it should dream deeply like that
of heavenly things.

TRANSLATED BY *Gail Holst-Warhaft*

20th Day, or The Little Phrase

The sun is like a mirror today
now that the spots from the back have passed
to the front and a dull shape stands
in the place of the image.
The refreshing content of vegetation
the demonstrations of emotions
and the lovely embellishments of decay,
all exhaust this hour
that resembles, in its stillness,
an animal sniffing at its last moment,
even though it doesn't know what God
might smell like!
And suddenly, in this soup of existence,
a little phrase rises to the froth
from the sludgy depths of dreams.
Unexpected, forgotten, flirtatious, childlike
with the sounds unspoiled by time,
a little June-bug phrase
comes through the open window:
"Ollie-ollie-oxen-free!"

TRANSLATED BY *Gail Holst-Warhaft*

Days Later, or The Moral Always in Prose

I look back at the war poems and see that the pain of others has become my own myth. Only now has my inner life come back with her suitcases full of impressions. But why was I in such a hurry to write down my objections to the horrifying and distant things that were happening at that time?

It is because my hidden self had stopped telling tales to my outside self. All my stories sail around in me like bodiless heads, sail around in a colorless essence which is not even oblivion.

Who went where and made fate turn sour? Who unbuttoned his shirt? Who bolted the gate?

How come I can't narrate in real time all these visitations of death?

I've immersed myself in foreign military operations because in my heart the traces of my last passionate campaign have been lost.

Athens, January 1991

TRANSLATED BY *Gail Holst-Warhaft*

FLUFFY THINGS

Out of the river-sheet, the lava-blanket,
the silence steeped in green eyes,
time piled up piecemeal inside me
shattered only by the ambiguity of the erotic moment—
from all that well-being
what moves me is the memory
of the fluffy bit in the belly button.
You should have seen it then
as if it had descended from the cloud
of another kind of truth, trapped
and waiting for the finger of a dark life
—my own—to free it
from the prison of the flesh
so it could be reunited
for no reason
with all the fluffy things that fly and stand up and rejoice
for no reason.
"There's no such thing as a face," they say
as they go in and out of nights and yesterdays
they have no idea what someone else's life means,
so specific, so overwhelming;
they only become visible for a second in the belly button
for no reason
and they have no idea what body or past means either
no idea at all . . .

TRANSLATED BY *Karen Van Dyck*

FLESH IS A BEAUTIFUL DESERT

THE OTHER PENELOPE

Penelope emerges from the olive trees
her hair more or less tidy
her dress from the neighborhood market
navy blue with white flowers.
She tells us it wasn't obsession
with the idea of "Odysseus"
that pressed her to let the suitors
wait for years in the forecourts
of her body's secret habits.
There in the island's palace—
with the fake horizons
of a saccharine love
and only the bird in the window
comprehending the infinite—
she had painted with nature's colors
the portrait of love.
Seated, one leg crossed over the other,
holding a cup of coffee
up early, a little grumpy, smiling a little
he emerges warm from the down of sleep.
His shadow on the wall:
trace of a piece of furniture just taken away
blood of an ancient murder
a lone performance of Karaghiozi
on the screen, pain always behind him.
Love and pain indivisible
like the pail and the child
on the sandy beach
the ah! and a crystal glass that slipped from one's hand
the green fly and the slaughtered animal
the soil and the shovel
the naked body and the single sheet in July.

And Penelope who now hears
the evocative music of fear
the cymbals of resignation
the sweet song of a quiet day
without sudden changes of weather and tone
the complex chords
of an infinite gratitude
for what did not happen, was not said, cannot be uttered
now signals no, no, no more loving
no more words and whispers
caresses and bites
small cries in the darkness
scent of flesh that burns in the light.
Pain was the most exquisite suitor
and she slammed the door on him.

TRANSLATED BY *Edmund and Mary Keeley*

THE TRANSCRIPTION OF A NIGHTMARE

For a nightmare to become a poem
the silence must be undisturbed by creakings
of the soul, the heart or other organs
of the inorganic chemistry of existence.
The silence may be occupied by colors
but striking clashes are forbidden:
black with rose
or with the much-sung blue of eyes.
Perhaps a bit of earthy brown
the bronze of a withered leaf
or white with brownish spots from a dog's neck.
Once the nightmare has reached its full height
it must undergo a series of operations.
With great dexterity every trace
of reasonable doubt must be removed
and then without anesthesia
something of inborn human kindness
must be transplanted there.
The most difficult surgery
is to cut it away from fear.
This you achieve by immersing
the bad dream unremittingly
in the holiness of nature.
And then the poem springs up;
leaf by tiny leaf
blossom by blossom
quite frail at first, trembling
it rises from the black earth that nourished it
and dares.
It dares to dream
the antidote for agony
the Word.

TRANSLATED BY *Jane Assimakopoulos*

LOVE-STRUCK REPTILE

Love-struck reptile
inside your domicile of flesh
I will crawl on my rubble-belly
to the crack where just a drop of light filters in
from the spreading blue of your eyes.
The worst part is not my life of dust
nor the darkness I begin to ape
nor the steady buzzing in my ears
like bees who have abandoned
two dead lovers
and are now flying off
with the passion of those two poor souls;
it's not that desire has begun to look
like a batty old lady
dressing up her unsavory tits
in a lace tablecloth
believing she's about to be married

        it's that
I dare, fallen creature that I am,
to dream that I have tiny legs and wings
that I can do somersaults and turns in the air
and that clearings of freshness exist in future days.

TRANSLATED BY *Jane Assimakopoulos*

Lipiu

Prologue

Poems fail
when loves fail,
don't listen to what they say:
a poem needs love's heat
to survive
cold time . . .

I've invented a place
to go when I am sad,
sad as the unmelting ice inside me,
sad as the crystallized tears,
when the regrets emerge, small white panther cubs
that nip and their bites sting.
Lipiu is what I call the place I've invented
to go when I am sad,
a state increasingly more intense
since all the dressed-up landscapes of the end
begin to smell of stagnant water
and rotten fruit.

You arrive in Lipiu without a sigh
only a slight tightening
like love standing
indecisive at the door.
Here you find cloud-stepping poets,
poets with an aptitude for heaven
who, towering high, nod as if to say
"No, must be a mistake," or "What a shame, too late now!"
while a beggar in the corner keeps murmuring:
"The good thing about desire
is that when it disappears

the value of the desired object
disappears too."

Here all of youth's failures
have become silent public squares
the crippled passions, dark groves
and the last pathetic love affairs,
unfed dogs who wander the back streets.
Something worse than old age,
this place is inhabited by wasted youth.

In Lipiu I cry all the time
ever since you showed me the value of sadness.
No, it's not the absence of fertility
but the positive image of absence . . .
You spoke and your profile startled me
as if carved in the hardest stone
and your eyes made of sulfur
in shock, shocked me.
So let's cry and call it joy
joy because we are still here suffering.
At daybreak we will enter another harbor
like entering a new poem
and in the early morning mist I'll hold
the last line of an untold love story.
Your voice, the curve of your neck, the height of your body,
the eternal repetition of an insatiable fear.
Looking at you I discovered
the hinterland of feeling.

The handsomest man in Lipiu
found a dead black butterfly in his sheets.
He was naked, sweating a little, and he gleamed

but not so brightly as the butterfly,
with all the unfathomable light
that came from death.
The butterfly, winged symbol of superficiality,
motionless, wearing the colors of night
was laid out on the bed as if death
had enjoyed her and then immediately abandoned her.
Or as if she were resting before setting off
on her difficult journey from blackness to perfection.

I'm the youngest woman in Lipiu.
I look and look and can't believe
that so much dust has piled up
on the road to joy.
I tell myself there must be some mistake
that I never managed to follow the silk route
or touch the poem's hero on the chest.
I only imagined his heart standing there
like the banks we walk by and say:
"Imagine the things locked up inside, imagine the riches!"

What you lose stays with you forever
and Lipiu is a place I created
so I can be with all the things I've lost
when those unbearable nightfalls take over
those voiceless daybreaks
and you're waiting for the school bell
to ring, and lessons to start again
one more unknown text to translate.
You look down at the courtyard, the gravel,
brush a few crumbs from your blue uniform
and enter the classroom;
enter the monotony of chalky time,

the vagueness of existence
which I know one finds again,
slightly altered, toward the end.

Religion in Lipiu
is a Headless Meaning.
Her statue stands obediently
next to those of her sisters:
Virtue, the most beautiful, and Wisdom
the one with perfect proportions.
Meaning, however, is worshipped headless
and when the one I would love if only . . .
kneels before her, wearing a pink shirt,
he is visibly aroused
because everything means something to him,
as well as its opposite.
Here love and death became one
and the grass that grows
between the statues' scattered limbs
gives them the appearance of living souls
who grieve amidst the green and wreck their ships
on foreign eyes and suffer love.
In Lipiu love-death is worshipped as one
without a head because it is without hope.

Exit

Leaving Lipiu behind
I understood that I had lost my orientation
toward something with a real smell,
the wrist's tender skin with the lovely pulse.
I took a walk around myself
and though heading for the boat
ended up in front of a locked-up store.
Behind the windowpane black with dust
a tragic jacket hung: no one
would ever wear its warmth.
The sun had set
and all the streets began
to howl in unison "No Way Out."
Cupping my hands
as though holding the final breath
of a frozen bird, I left
protecting the last handshake.

TRANSLATED BY *Karen Van Dyck*

NEW POEMS

"Hush Now, Don't Be Afraid . . ."

"Hush now, don't be afraid . . ."
we are the voices of old loves
not the voices that changed your life
so you suddenly found yourself in other rooms
worshipping other statues.
But the little loves
that for only one second
made you look up high
with heavenly familiarity
while some unruly leafy plant
a giggle, a glance
made you forget the evergreen thorns
of cactus time.
Little love of the last minute,
lean on a shoulder
fanatically mortal
lean on the cenotaph of dreams.

TRANSLATED BY *Karen Van Dyck*

MATTER ALONE

I take a thing and change its place.
I'm not sure why, but it bothered me.
Seconds later
the cloth, the paper
lets out a whisper-cry
as matter shifts.
Does this imperceptible sound
express discomfort or relief
with this new configuration
of the infinite and the inanimate?
Or is it that the object
longs for home?
A tiny little movement,
a glance, a spark of light
and an inner self springs up
moving freely
in an absent-minded now.
Something like erotic murmuring
or the cry of a hungry dog.
"That's how matter alone must sound," I say
before another silence, my own,
snatches me up.

Aegina, 11 August 1999

TRANSLATED BY *Karen Van Dyck*

POETRY GUIDED ME WELL

Poetry guided me well
straight into you
with a brim-full darkness
blinding me like lightning.
I never erred
for the words came
from within the shameless
desperation
of your fickle touch
and the eggshell of knowledge
broke with a crack
there inside the wall
of the thorax.
Steeped in verbs
I foresaw your movements
before you completed them in the air
while the divine adjective
chose the colors
before you wore them.
Oh! How lovely it was back then
when I would miss you
and you were ever-present in the poem
where I created you
and you me
eternally sad!
But poetry can sense
when you're out to wear her down
when emotion grows hard
with passion
and turns into a whip
and gives pain.
The poem then withdraws
from sorrow's

uncomfortable seating
and I'm left alone in dreadful company:
the voiceless object
or your glossy-eyed gaze
with the few bits of flesh
that cover the wilderness
of your soul
and your ankles once
shining landmarks
for poets in the night.

TRANSLATED BY *Jane Assimakopoulos*

LIPIU ONCE AGAIN

Silence is the language of Lipiu

Prologue

As with love
poems are born
in silence
only that unfeeling silence
has a habit
of giving birth
and swallowing its young.

1

In Lipiu you study silence
as if it were a foreign language
if you practice enough
you can tell the dialect
of day from the heavy accent
of night.
You learn the birds by heart
and the light that alters
the meaning of nothing.
You will never be able
to express yourself freely in this language
but you will always be surprised by its truth.
You read the trees, the mountains in the original.
You ask: What do I have to say in this language?
The wounded animal deep inside you doesn't answer.
It remains silent.

2

Today the rain broke out
in a flood of incomprehensible curses.
On the TV screen humans
move around without sound:
bodies, smiles, embraces,
handshakes, the tying of ties, punches . . .
I couldn't hear the words
and the bureaucracy of existence
seemed absurd.
Why, why him, the sweet, absent-minded one?
With what does passion agree?
It seems I have forgotten the syntax
of youth.

3

In the taverna garden
it is spring and the blossoming
chestnut trees lean attentively
over the pensioners.
Beards, mustaches, all white,
a little laughter in their faded
blue eyes peeking out behind the beer froth
the slender waitress
like a doll just out of her box
with the divine department store tag
still around her neck.
The brown spots on the old men's hands
—maps of an unknown geography—
the flowers scattered by the wind
on the wooden table

and suddenly I understood silence:
it is the womb of all languages.

4

It is the language of the beginning,
of the question when you search for the phrase
of leaves and you ask yourself what's the use
of so many daybreaks, so many breaths
so many cries smothered in the grass
what is this life for, how will I open the door?
Will I be accepted? How do I take
the first step in the rain alone
toward the first meeting
with the savior-destroyer?
Even the most beautiful imagination is useless
in the face of a pile of days
a shapeless pile, with no scent and no known meaning.

5

But silence is also
the mother tongue of the end
when you try to read the word EXIT
written in the darkness with tar
over a gate or maybe it's a burrow? a hole?
Are you going to emerge in pain
or in triumph
or will you have become a baby again,
carefree, sucking the breast-
clouds of the day?

Exit

In this languageless world
where I have come for mute studies
the exercises are deafening;
I know my silence
doesn't flow yet,
doesn't flow naturally.

Munich, May 2000

TRANSLATED BY *Karen Van Dyck*

Translating Life's End into Love

For P. S.

Because I cannot touch you
with my tongue
I transliterate my passion.
Because I cannot take your communion
I transubstantiate you.
Because I cannot undress you
I imagine you in the clothes
of a foreign language.
Because I cannot nestle
under your wing
I fly around you
turning the pages of your dictionary.
I want to learn how you bare yourself
how you open yourself up.
That's why I search
between the lines
for your habits
the fruits you love
the smells you prefer
the girls you leaf through.
Because I'll never see
your punctuation marks naked
I work hard on your adjectives
so I can recite them in another religion.
Now that my story's old
and my book's no longer on the shelf
it's you I imagine
in a rare leather binding
with gold lettering
in a foreign library.
Because I should never have given in

to the indulgence of nostalgia
and written this poem
I read the gray sky
in a sun-drenched translation.

Rhodes, 16 March 2002

TRANSLATED BY *Karen Van Dyck*

NOTES

Penelope Says
Daniel Weissbort is a contemporary English poet who taught for
thirty years at the University of Iowa and was founding editor of
the journal *Modern Poetry in Translation.*

Aegina
A Greek island in the Saronic Gulf near Athens. It is the poet's sum-
mer home.

The Wedding
This poem was written on the occasion of the editor's wedding in
Pelion.

Springtime for Yanousa
The name Yanousa is a made-up, feminine version of Anghelaki-
Rooke's father's name, Yannos.

War Diary
These poems were written in 1991 during the first Gulf War. Pedro
Matteo is a Spanish poet who lives in Greece.

The Other Penelope
Karaghiozi is the Greek shadow puppet of Turkish origin who over-
comes adversity through humor.

Lipiu
The title comes from the Greek word for sadness *(lípi)* and the
Romanian ending *-u* (as in Sibiu and Ceauşescu) and refers to a
place full of sadness. The poem was composed at a poetry festival
in Constanţa, Romania in 1995, coincidentally where Ovid wrote
his *Tristia.*

"Hush Now, Don't Be Afraid . . ."
The title is a quotation from a poem, "The Fates" *(I Moíres),* by the
Greek poet Kostis Palamas (1859–1943). My translation borrows
from Stephanos Papadopoulos's translation of this title "Hush,
Don't Be Afraid."

Translating Life's End into Love
The initials P. S. stand for Panos Stathogiannis, a contemporary
Greek writer.

Editor's Acknowledgments

This project has been made possible by funding from the Greek Ministry of Culture and the Lodge Foundation. I am grateful for their generous support.

The cover illustration of Katerina Anghelaki-Rooke as Penelope was a present from the artist Alekos Fasianos.

I am particularly thankful for the valuable insights and advice of Rodney Rooke, Katerina Anghelaki-Rooke's husband. He always managed to find the right word in English for Katerina's Greek when everyone else had given up hope. I am sad that he did not live to see the completion of this project.

I would like to thank Laurie Hart, who was as eager to see this collection in print as I was and who sat in on many editorial sessions, offering her thoughtful suggestions and using her veto power judiciously. I am also indebted to Fay Zika, whose other red house in Aegina was as much the home of this labor as the poet's, and whose clear-sightedness improved the manuscript immensely.

I would like to thank Olga Broumas, Dianne Chisholm, Pellegrino D'Acierno, John Davis, Jonathan Galassi, Ekaterini Douka-Kabitoglou, Stathis Gourgouris, Maria Margaronis, Jonathan Walker and Elizabeth Young-Bruehl for their encouragement along the way. Peter Constantine, Rachel Hadas, and Clair Wills have my gratitude for their comments on the final manuscript, and Patricia Storace for her generous resourcefulness, which helped this manuscript reach the right publisher.

I want to thank my editors Peter Jay at Anvil and Jeffrey Shotts at Graywolf who make publishing poetry not only possible but a joyous endeavor. I am also particularly grateful to Karen Emmerich whose thoughtful editing and insight are present throughout this book, and also to Lytton Jackson Smith for his help with proofing this edition. As always I am indebted to Nelson Moe for his clear sense of what a poem is and for his persuasive vision of less as more. And, finally, I am most indebted to the poet herself for the care and rigor she put into this project, and to all the poetry readers who have insisted over the years that we need more poetry in English by Katerina Anghelaki-Rooke.

Karen Van Dyck

Permission Acknowledgments

For permission to include previously published translations in this collection, grateful acknowledgment is made to:

Associated University Presses for the translations by Rae Dalven from *Daughters of Sappho* (Fairleigh Dickinson University Press, 1994).

The Attika Tradition Foundation, Athens, for the translations by Kimon Friar.

BOA Editions for "I Have a Stone," "Heat," "My Plastic Thing," "Writing," "Beings and Things on Their Own," and "The Barber Shop" from *Beings and Things on Their Own* translated by Katerina Anghelaki-Rooke with Jackie Willcox. Copyright © 1986 by Katerina Anghelaki-Rooke. Reprinted with the permission of BOA Editions, Ltd., www.boaeditions.org

Shoestring Press for poems included in *From Purple into Night*, copyright © 1987 Katerina Anghelaki-Rooke and Jackie Willcox.

"War Diary" first appeared in *Modern Poetry in Translation*, New Series No. 6, Winter 1994–5. "Jealousy" first appeared in *Translation*, vol. XIV, Spring 1985. "Lipiu," "Hush Now, Don't Be Afraid," "Matter Alone," and "Lipiu Once Again" appeared in *A Century of Greek Poetry: 1900–2000*, eds. Peter Bien, Peter Constantine, Edmund Keeley, Karen Van Dyck (River Vale, NJ: Cosmos, 2004).

Other translations by Jane Assimakopoulos, Gail Holst-Warhaft, Edmund and Mary Keeley, Karen Van Dyck, and Jackie Willcox in collaboration with Katerina Anghelaki-Rooke are reprinted by kind permission of the author and translators.

About the Poet and the Translators

KATERINA ANGHELAKI-ROOKE was born in Athens in 1939. She studied foreign languages and literature at the universities of Nice, Athens, and Geneva. In 1962 she was awarded the First Prize for Poetry of the City of Geneva. She received two grants from the Ford Foundation (1972, 1975), as well as the Greek National Prize for Poetry (1985) and the Greek Academy's Poetry Prize (2000). She attended the International Writing Program at the University of Iowa in 1974–75 and was a Fulbright Visiting Lecturer at Harvard, Utah, and San Francisco State Universities in 1982, as well as a Fellow at the Program in Hellenic Studies at Princeton in 1987. She has published fourteen books of poetry as well as four collected volumes. She is fluent in English, French, and Russian and is an acclaimed translator of Seamus Heaney and Alexander Pushkin, among others. Her work has been translated into French, German, Italian, Spanish, Swedish, Polish, Serbian, Dutch, Bulgarian, Hebrew, and English.

JANE ASSIMAKOPOULOS is an American writer and translator living in Ioannina, Greece. Her translations include novels by award-winning writers Thanassis Valtinos (Northwestern University Press) and Michel Fais (University of Birmingham Press), as well as poems and stories in literary journals and anthologies. She is also a translation editor overseeing the Greek translation of Philip Roth's novels.

RAE DALVEN was born in Preveza, Greece, and moved to New York at the age of five. Her life work was the translation of Greek poetry into English with special attention to the poetry of women. Her translation of C. P. Cavafy introduced by W. H. Auden is still in print today. Her *Daughters of Sappho* (1994) is the most comprehensive anthology of contemporary Greek women poets available.

She retired from her professorship in the English Department at Ladycliff College, Highland Falls, New York, in 1974 and died in 1992.

KIMON FRIAR was born in Imrali, Turkey, in 1911 to an American father and a Greek mother. His anthology *Modern Poetry: British and American* (with John Malcolm Brinnin) helped establish the canon of twentieth-century literature in English. His translation of Nikos Kazantzakis's *The Odyssey: A Modern Sequel* appeared to great critical acclaim in 1958. His anthology *Modern Greek Poetry: from Cavafis to Elytis* (1975) introduced English readers to a broad range of contemporary Greek poets. Friar received the Greek World Award (1978), a Ford Foundation Grant (1986), and a National Foundation of the Arts Grant (1986). He died in Athens in 1993.

GAIL HOLST-WARHAFT was born in Melbourne, Australia. She divides her time as a poet, translator, and adjunct professor in Classics and Comparative Literature at Cornell University. Her books include *Road to Rembetika: Music of Greek Subculture* (1975). *Theodorakis: Myth and Politics in Modern Greek Music* (1980), *Dangerous Voices: Women's Laments and Greek Literature* (1992), and *The Cue for Passion: Grief and Its Political Uses* (2000). She has published translations of Aeschylus, Iakovos Kambanellis, Nikos Kavvadias, and Alki Zei.

EDMUND KEELEY is the author of seven novels, ten volumes of nonfiction, and fifteen volumes of poetry in translation. He taught English, Creative Writing, and Hellenic Studies at Princeton University for forty years, and retired as Straut Professor of English. His latest books are a literary history, *Inventing Paradise: The Greek Journey, 1937–47* (1999, 2002), a novel, *Some Wine for Remembrance* (2001), and a memoir, *Borderlines* (2005). His awards include the Rome Prize and the Award in Literature from the American Academy of Arts and Letters, the Landon Translation Award from the Academy of American Poets, and the PEN/Ralph Manheim Medal for Translation.

MARY KEELEY is a freelance translator who has often collaborated with her husband, Edmund Keeley, in rendering individual poems. Her book-length translations are Vassilis Vassilikos's *The Plant, the Well, the Angel and The Monarch,* as well as Katie Katsoyannis's *Correspondence with Dimitri Mitropoulos.*

KAREN VAN DYCK is the Kimon A. Doukas Professor of Modern Greek Literature and the Director of the Program in Hellenic Studies at Columbia University, where she teaches courses on Modern Greek culture, Diaspora, gender, and translation. Her publications include *Kassandra and the Censors: Greek Poetry since 1967* (1998; Greek translation, 2002), *The Rehearsal of Misunderstanding: Three Collections by Contemporary Greek Women Poets* (1998), and the co-edited anthology, *A Century of Greek Poetry, 1900–2000* (2004).

JACKIE WILLCOX is Secretary and Librarian of the Russian and Eurasian Studies Centre at St Antony's College, Oxford. Her published translations from Modern Greek include two volumes of poetry by Katerina Anghelaki-Rooke, *Beings and Things on Their Own* and *From Purple into Night* (both with the poet), Costas Taktsis's "A Story of Diplomacy," and Yorgos Ioannou's "Good Friday Vigil" (both with Peter Mackridge), as well as poems by Haris Vlavianos.

THE LANNAN TRANSLATION SERIES

Funding the translation and publication of exceptional literary works

The Scattered Papers of Penelope by Katerina Anghelaki-Rooke,
edited and translated from the Greek by Karen Van Dyck

The Accordionist's Son by Bernardo Atxaga,
translated from the Spanish by Margaret Jull Costa

The Lovers of Algeria by Anouar Benmalek,
translated from the French by Joanna Kilmartin

The Star of Algiers by Aziz Chouaki,
translated from the French by Ros Schwartz and Lulu Norman

A House at the Edge of Tears by Vénus Khoury-Ghata,
translated from the French by Marilyn Hacker

Nettles by Vénus Khoury-Ghata,
translated from the French by Marilyn Hacker

She Says by Vénus Khoury-Ghata,
translated from the French by Marilyn Hacker

A Wake for the Living by Radmila Lazic,
translated from the Serbian by Charles Simic

No Shelter by Pura López-Colomé,
translated from the Spanish by Forrest Gander

New European Poets,
edited by Wayne Miller and Kevin Prufer

Look There by Agi Mishol, translated from the Hebrew by Lisa Katz

Out Stealing Horses by Per Petterson,
translated from the Norwegian by Anne Born

To Siberia by Per Petterson,
translated from the Norwegian by Anne Born

Shyness and Dignity by Dag Solstad,
translated from the Norwegian by Sverre Lyngstad

Meanwhile Take My Hand by Kirmen Uribe,
translated from the Basque by Elizabeth Macklin

Without an Alphabet, Without a Face by Saadi Youssef,
translated from the Arabic by Khaled Mattawa

The Scattered Papers of Penelope is set in Arno Pro, a face designed by Robert Slimbach and named after the river that runs through Florence. This book was designed by Ann Sudmeier. Composition by BookMobile Design and Publishing Services, Minneapolis, Minnesota, and manufactured by Versa Press on acid-free paper.